To Pamela, my sister in Christ, may our Daddy bless you and give you favor! ♡

Joyfully,
Jeanette
8/23/2020

GIRL DISTORTED JOY RESTORED
Journey to Innocent Again

JEANETTE FINN

Copyright © 2019 Jeanette Finn

All rights reserved.

Published by Author Academy Elite

P.O. Box 43, Powell, OH 43035

ISBN 978-1-64085-397-3 (paperback)

ISBN 978-1-64085-398-0 (hardback)

ISBN 978-1-64085-399-7 (ebook)

Library of Congress Control Number (LCCN): 2018953533

All rights reserved. No part of this publication may be reproduced, stored in a retrieval system, or transmitted in any form or by any means—electronic, mechanical, photocopy, recording, or any other—except for brief quotations in printed reviews, without the prior permission of the publisher.

Printed in the United States of America

For those who desire to be Innocent Again

Table of Contents

Introduction ix

Part 1 Innocence Stolen

That Night 1
The Next Morning. 4
I Lied to the Police 6
Why He Did It 10
He's Baaaack 13
Dad's Proposition 16
Business Trip to CA 19
The Last Time. 25

Part 2 Impact Happens

Abuse Leads to Abuse. 31
Becoming a Call Girl 33
Marrying a Narcissist 36

Drinking is the Problem 39

Mom Knows 45

Mom Has a Secret. 50

I'll Kill Him 53

It Doesn't Have to be This Way. 55

It's an Internal Affair. 59

Drinking's Not the Only Problem. 63

Off and On the Wagon 67

Sober Again. 69

Replaced and Discarded 71

A Hurtful Divorce. 74

Pity Party. 77

Part 3 Inspiration Follows

Healing is a Process. 81

Relationships Take Work. 83

Renewing My Mind. 86

Releasing Guilt 90

Seeing Differently 93

Living in the Moment. 96

Wouldn't Change a Thing 99

Conclusion 103

Introduction

This is my journey to *Innocent Again*. It wasn't an easy story to write. At times, it was so difficult that I wondered why I even thought I could do it. For weeks at a time I would stop writing, but then the desire to help other survivors of sexual abuse always won out. I am not a counselor, so speaking about addictions, narcissism and healing comes from my own experiences, personal studies and perspective. You won't find any footnotes or quotes from professionals. This is purely me helping you. Although I have experienced hellish circumstances and situations, I have peace and joy in my life, and I can help you have it too.

For healing to begin, we must shine the light into the darkness. We must not have any secrets. Secrets keep us separated from each other, keep us feeling alone and keep us from being our true selves. Secrets cause us to wear masks. We discuss all kinds of sexual issues; it's time to discuss this one.

Incest, and more generally the sexual abuse of children, is so shameful and secretive that it is impossible to know the true statistics. The Child Molestation Research and Prevention Institute conservatively estimates that two in every ten little girls and one in every ten little boys are victims. They also claim there are 39 million adults who have survived child sexual abuse living in the United States.

I wrote this book to help those survivors and to bring awareness to the fact that those survivors need help. Most of them are just going through life, either not knowing about or not understanding the impact sexual abuse had (and still has) on them. Joy escapes them. They may be in harmful relationships or they may not be able to keep relationships. It may show up at work, making it difficult to get or keep jobs. They may be overweight, drinking, overspending or gambling to keep their shame at bay. Their pain needs to be talked about to be released.

I want this book to start that vital conversation. My journey and information is organized into three sections. Each section is in chronological order and has questions throughout for you to consider, helping you take the necessary steps on your own journey to Innocent Again.

Part 1 Innocence Stolen: I share what happened to me, in hopes that sharing my story will help you share yours. Our stories are different, yet the same.

Our innocence was ripped away from us. Our femininity, sexuality and trust were distorted to varying degrees and had an impact on the choices we would make in our lives – especially the choices of how we would treat our bodies and how we allowed others to treat our bodies.

Part 2 Impact Happens: Sexual abuse of any kind, especially on a minor, is going to have an impact on the way they perceive the world around them and the choices they make. Trust and sexuality both end up very distorted. I share several wrong decisions and life choices that I made as a child and well into my adult life because of incest. You will see how my inability to set boundaries and fight for them caused a lot of pain.

Part 3 Inspiration Follows: The only reason I wrote this book! You can overcome, you can be free, you can forgive and be forgiven…you can be Innocent Again! Sure, there are steps forward and then steps backwards, but any steps towards healing make you stronger.

The sections do not have to be read in order. Jumping right into Part 1, my story of abuse, might not be the best approach for you. Feel free to start in another section if you need to.

It doesn't matter how long the journey takes, just that you are on it. I know you are on it because you are reading this right now. Thank you for allowing me to share my journey with you. By doing so, I hope it helps move yours along with compassion, grace and hope.

Here's to you on your Journey to Innocent Again! Read on…

Part 1
INNOCENCE STOLEN

(When the natural development of sexuality is taken from a child)

That Night

I WAS ASLEEP. My Pippi Longstocking book lay open in my reading corner and my dollhouse family were all safely tucked in bed like I thought I was. My dad was drunk. I was a small, brown-haired, sound asleep ten-year-old. He slithered into my room and sexually assaulted me. My innocence was ripped away, stolen. I would no longer be able to experience the world as a little girl is meant to. There would be no innocence of discovery. There would be no joy of becoming a woman – only wishing I wasn't one. If only I had been born a boy like my dad wanted. My whole world was irrevocably changed that night.

I really struggled with how much to share about what happened during that first sexual assault. My original draft was graphically detailed, even down to the sounds I remembered. Through the process of writing this book I heard the phrase "honesty with modesty." It was in a video I watched, and the lady was talking about sexual abuse she experienced in her childhood. At the time I was very annoyed. Why isn't she saying who did it or what exactly happened? I felt like she was just copping out and wondered if she hadn't fully healed since she wasn't saying who or what.

As she continued to talk about the many things she had lost because of what happened, it hit me. I had lost those very same things; the same things everyone who has been sexually abused has lost. Tears started flowing. The truth is, the specific details of what happened or who did it doesn't matter. Any form of sexual abuse on a minor creates the same loss. This truth impacted me so much that I removed that entire graphic section from my manuscript.

I also learned that sometimes if you are talking about specific sex acts, you may be sexually arousing someone. That is the *last* thing I want to do in this arena! Sufficient to say, things were done to me as a child that should never be done to a child.

Another reason I don't share what my dad did to me is because I don't know your reason for picking up this taboo-topic book. It could be for any number of reasons. Maybe you have a friend or family member who this happened to and you want to better understand how you can help them. Maybe a friend or family member gave it to you. Maybe you have wounds in the process of healing. Maybe you don't remember if something happened to you but suspect something.

You don't need to read about specifics, especially because specifics don't matter. Any form of inappropriate sexual contact or interaction (visual, verbal or psychological) is harmful to children. Their view of sexuality, trust and sense of security become distorted. Healing from incest and sexual abuse from childhood is a very difficult process and impossible to do alone.

There is definitely a time to talk about your specifics with a safe person. I have shared details in a safe place with safe people when appropriate. Getting it out of your head and through your mouth is part of the healing process. If you don't talk about what happened to you with someone, then it stays stuck rolling around in your head. It's still a secret and secrets keep you from joy. Light must be shined into the darkness.

Do you agree there is a time and a place to share?
Do you have a safe place to share?
Have you ever told anyone?
Did they believe you?

The Next Morning

SITTING IN MY fifth-grade classroom the next morning was surreal. I looked around the classroom at each student as I waited for class to start. As I surveyed each kid as they sat at their desks, I was convinced they would suddenly notice something different about me. I felt so dirty, like that character in Charlie Brown called Pigpen. Wherever he walked a cloud of dirt surrounded him. *There must be something like that surrounding me now.* But as I looked at them, they didn't seem to see anything different about me. I began wondering if it had ever happened to anyone else, because if it had I probably wouldn't be able to tell either. Realizing someone else could be sitting there with that same secret was horrifying. That really scared me. I could no longer trust anything or anyone. Things are not what they seem.

Joy Restored

Statistically speaking, it is highly likely there were at least two other kids in that classroom who had the same secret. I knew I would keep my secret because I had already learned that you don't involve other people, even the police, in your life when you are scared or confused. If you did, something worse could happen. Keeping the secret seemed like the only option.

I Lied to the Police

BEFORE THAT LIFE-CHANGING night, when I was eight years old, I had decided to stay home when my parents went to the grocery store. It was still light out, but I didn't consider that it wasn't going to stay light for much longer. The winter months in the Pacific Northwest get dark early. I am talking like dark at 5 p.m. It can be a very dreary time, especially when you add in the months of rain. Also, for an eight-year-old, it's a little spooky, especially because this was around Halloween.

It hadn't been dark for long, but I was getting really scared. The phone rang. I answered it. It was a really nice lady, probably a telemarketer. She asked me if my parents were home. I said no and started crying. She asked me how old I was and my address because she wanted to send help. I wanted to be helped and gave her my address.

Joy Restored

Only three states had laws regarding a minimum age for leaving a child home alone: Illinois, Maryland and Oregon. In Oregon, a child needed to be ten years old and I wasn't. With that in mind, you know who that nice lady called? The police.

My parents arrived home shortly after that call. I instantly ran and hugged my mom, crying, so happy she was home. Then, there was a knock on the door.

My dad pulled the curtains aside to peak out the window.

"It's the police," he said in such a way that made me feel scared. I thought *Oh no, what have I done?* I knew it had something to do with talking to that stranger.

He opened the door. The officers told him they had received a call that a child was home alone.

"No, we have been here all evening. You must have the wrong house," my dad said as he opened the door a little wider so the two policemen could see my mom and me standing there.

One of the policemen asked me from the doorway, "Have you been home alone?"

I shook my head no, because I knew that was what I was supposed to do. I was supposed to lie.

He asked me, "Are you sure everything is okay?"

I nodded my head yes.

"These are your parents?"

I nodded my head again.

They asked a few more questions of my dad, and then he shut the door, turned and glared at me.

"What did you do?" he asked.

I told him about the lady who called and how I gave her my name and address. After that, I got sat down and received quite the scary lecture…how I could have been hauled off, taken from my parents, how the police would have considered my parents unfit, and then I'd be put in the foster system. He was really trying to scare me, making the police out to be the bad guys. I started crying.

My mom tried to step in and make it less dramatic. My dad would have none of that. Looking back, I realize he saw this as a grooming opportunity (sex predators manipulate their victims to keep secrets). It wasn't a planned opportunity, like they usually are, but a perfect one nonetheless. He seized the incident, using it to get me to fear the police. He fed me instructions to lie to them in order to protect myself and my parents from them. Instead of seeing the police as people who could protect me, someone to turn to in time of need, I now saw them as the bad guys. My dad also knew now that I would lie for him.

This instinct of mine, or of any child, to protect my parents even if it meant lying and keeping secrets is a big part of why child abuse of any kind can happen. Fear is a secret's stronghold.

Were you told specifically to keep a secret, or did you just feel so dirty you didn't want to tell anyone?

Were you threatened or was someone you loved threatened if you didn't keep the secret?

Why He Did It

THE FIRST TIME my dad and I were alone after the night he sexually assaulted me, he explained to me why he did what he did. He told me, "Sex is the most important thing in a marriage. If your mom wasn't so good at it, I wouldn't still be married to her." He told me about orgasms and that, since I didn't have one, there might be something wrong with me. He did give me what seemed like good news at the time: sneaking into my bedroom in the middle of the night wasn't going to happen again. The bad news though, was that he would wait till I was more mature, and then I would want it. Keep in mind, I was only ten years old. I thought to myself, *I am never going to want it, but if you say I am going to want it…it will never be from you! Maybe my husband someday, but never you.*

He then showed me a vibrator. It was old. He turned it on and there was the smell of something burning. You slipped your hand into it and the motor sat on top of your hand and your hand would vibrate. I was supposed to use this whenever I wanted, so I could learn how to experience pleasure "down there" because something might be wrong with me.

Confusion swirled in my thoughts because I had some strange feelings during the assault that might have felt good. I didn't want it to feel good. I knew it was wrong. I willed the sensations to go away. During the assault, I ended up with what is referred to as an "out of body experience." I left my body. I was above my body in the farthest corner of the room, right over the top of my dollhouse, looking down. I was trying desperately to will my body to not feel. After his talk, I had the idea that someday this might be okay, but not now, not with him.

I was so mortified knowing my dad would be watching me turn into a woman, and at some point, would try to do those things to me again. When would he sneak in my room again? At what age would he consider me to be his victim again? What a horrible, haunting, taunting cloud to have looming over me. Growing up, developing breasts, getting my period – these are in themselves difficult and big transitions, let alone with a predator lurking down the hall.

As I write this, I gain another layer of compassion for myself and the decisions I made as an adult. As you take this journey to Innocent Again, you will develop compassion for yourself. As you understand your story and its impact on how you made decisions and the things you did, you will be able to forgive yourself. You were a child. You did nothing to deserve that abuse. You did the best you could with the information you had at the time.

Do you need to forgive yourself?

Do you have compassion for yourself?

He's Baaaack

I LOST MY virginity at 15. Isn't that funny how we say *lost*? I didn't lose it. I know exactly where I was and who I let take it. It was my sophomore boyfriend, my freshman year of high school. My folks found out I was sexually active because of a piece of condom wrapper left on the floor of their bedroom. I think I felt compelled to have sex on their bed to spite my dad, or in an attempt to feel like my sexuality was my own. It wasn't though; it was already distorted.

It was distorted by those five years of him lurking around, watching me mature. Those years were full of inappropriate grabbing – of me and the way he would grab my mom in front of me and so many other things, like the shows we would watch on TV, the conversations that took place and the treatment of women as sex objects (which our whole society is so guilty of doing). Even if you haven't been physically sexually abused, you have been emotionally sexually abused by American society. It's an epidemic. The distortion between femininity and sexuality is huge. That may be my next book: *Femininity Distorted*.

Apparently, my dad's thought process was now that I was not a virgin, it was time to approach me again. This shows the patience, cunning and planning of a predator.

My dad started sharing secrets with me about people I knew or had known, like the mom of two boys I used to babysit and how Dad got her to have sex with my cousin when he was 13 and she was almost 30. How he had a threesome with her and her husband. How the husband of another friend of the family would have his wife lie completely still when they had sex because he wanted to 'do it with a dead person.' How my dad and my Uncle Phil had a secret apartment where they took young girls and had sex. The web of sex and secrets was being wrapped around me.

The thing is, stories like this are enticing. You know how it is…someone asks if you can keep a secret and you want to hear it. Someone says, "I have a secret" and you want to hear it. Keeping secrets separates you from others. It makes you feel special. We are all predisposed to wanting to feel *special*. This desire within all of us is why abuse of all kinds continues.

He told me these secrets over the course of a few weeks. I felt safer with him than I had in a long time.

Joy Restored

It was like I was his equal now that I was having sex, and we shared this secret world. It didn't seem like he was setting me up to have sex with him, but that's what predators do. They stalk their prey. They have a plan. It's all a set up.

Were you groomed by your offender?

Or was it something that happened because you were just there and vulnerable?

Dad's Proposition

MY DAD APPROACHED me now that he had his new strategy in play. He would keep telling me more private secrets about people, me and Kevin (my boyfriend) could have a key to the secret apartment to use whenever we wanted, and he would buy me a car when I turned 16… *if* I would have sex with him, *if* we would have a secret little affair ourselves.

I said, "No way. I have a boyfriend. I am not a cheater!"

He said, "Ask him. Tell him everything I have offered you and he'll say yes. Kevin will agree to it. Ask him. You'll see."

I said, "No he won't. He loves me. He wants me all to himself."

My dad already had Kevin pegged.

He said again, "Ask him, you'll see."

My dad approved of Kevin right from the beginning. He was tall, athletic and good looking. He called

Joy Restored

him 'good breeding stock.' I am serious – that is how he referred to my choices in boyfriends, if they were good breeding stock or not. I suppose that's where I got it in my head that you didn't just fall in love with someone, but that you could choose who you fell in love with. Kevin also liked my dad. In general, my friends liked my dad. He was fun. He was an adult that acted like a kid and treated kids like adults.

I told Kevin about my dad's offer. He thought it sounded pretty good! *OMG! So much for love.* He wanted to know where the secret apartment was to help us make our decision. It was so humiliating to ask my Dad for the address, admitting to him that Kevin was actually considering this. It was one of the units of a 6-plex he and my uncle had built. It was in that parking lot where Kevin tried to convince me that my dad's offer wasn't that bad.

"I mean, he is going to get you a car in a few months when you turn 16 and we could drive over here, and it would be like our own little place. We could have sex whenever we want."

After that, I broke up with Kevin. I was devastated. My dad was right. How did he know Kevin would agree? *Maybe it was true that all this love stuff was crap and it's all about the sex.* After that, a really sad turn of events happened for me, but I handled it to the best of my ability with the knowledge and experience I had up to that point in my life.

That's what we do, right? We handle things to the best of our ability with the knowledge gained from the environment we grew up in. That is why it is so important to have grace for yourself and others. We don't know what we don't know. We can't make a better choice without better information. That is why getting information and learning is so important. It's a lifelong process.

Most of our learning as adults is going to be *unlearning* – tearing down misinformation and wrong beliefs. As children we are like sponges soaking everything up. Sadly, a lot of the things we soak up are not from healthy people. We didn't get to choose the environment we grew up in and that environment impacts us more than we'd like to admit.

Did someone who should have protected you from your abuser fail you?

Have you taken the time to notice how your childhood impacts your life?

Business Trip to CA

MY PARENTS HAD started their own company: it was called U.S. Consumer. One of the product lines was transparent stickers that were put on windows, mostly the back windows of cars. It was thriving. We had the opportunity to have display racks in the 7-Eleven stores along the West Coast, which was quite an accomplishment.

At this point, we needed to get the display racks picked up and fast. The one time run that 7-Eleven let us have was done. That was the deal: a one-time run, and then we had to pick up the racks and any unsold merchandise. My dad kept putting it off. He thought he could manipulate their whole system. His strategy was to not pick up the racks, assuming they would then give in and say, "Okay, let's order more stickers from U.S. Consumer since we do still have their racks."

He was always thinking he could change the system. But it didn't work, and now 7-Eleven had threatened to destroy whatever was not picked up. The racks alone were worth thousands of dollars, let alone any leftover product. That is how we ended up with the very unplanned and *must get done quickly* trip to CA. The fastest and cheapest way possible meant us driving down there in our cargo van and loading them up ourselves, which was no small feat.

Here's where it became personal for me. My folks weren't going to leave me home for three nights on my own. I was a sexually active teenage girl with a boyfriend. I assured them I had broken up with him and gave my dad the evil eye. My mom didn't believe it and thought that I just wanted to be alone with Kevin. Next, I tried to have it be just me and my mom to go, but my dad would have none of that. It wasn't safe for us girls. *Not safe for us girls? What about not safe for me?!* Of course, he wouldn't let this opportunity pass him by. Three nights alone on the road with his 15-year-old daughter. This couldn't have worked out better if he'd planned it.

I felt stuck. I could either tell my mom what had happened, what was happening and what would happen, or I could go on the trip with my dad. I knew what would happen. I knew what I was getting myself into. That's why when it came to the healing process of incest, I had a very hard time with not blaming myself for what happened to me. I had chosen to go; I chose not to speak up.

Feeling responsible for what happened to them is very common for victims of sexual abuse. Releasing that responsibility is one of the first steps in healing. It was a very hard step for me...but I am getting ahead of myself.

If I told my mom everything that had happened—the proposition dad made me and Kevin, which was why Kevin and I had broken up—I knew I wouldn't have to go to CA with Dad. I knew my mom would leave my dad. She would believe me. My mom knew my dad had cheated on her more than once. Being aware of him abusing me was something she wouldn't stand for, but I didn't know what would happen after that. Maybe she'd go back to Germany where all her family was?

Besides, I was disgusted with my mom at that point in my life. I couldn't understand why she wouldn't leave him, especially after I told her I would help her leave him. I offered to get a job after school and help pay rent. *Do I give her another reason to leave him?* She already had plenty without having to know about the incest. We were both alone and stuck dealing with this sexual narcissistic predator.

Have you made decisions that weren't in your best interest because you didn't know what would happen?

Have you ever made a decision to *not* help someone else because you didn't think they deserved it?

It looked like I would be going on a road trip with Dad. The first night, just over the state line of CA, we stopped for the night. Thinking about it now conjures up such ugly feelings. The good news is nothing happened that night except for him making me come to bed naked. How I can say that was "the good news" is sad. He spooned into me with his nakedness, while I lay in fear and disgust of what may happen next. He assured me nothing more was going to happen. We were just going to lay together. I tried to believe him and go to sleep. Nothing more happened that night.

On the second night, we stayed in another cheap hotel near the place where we were picking up the racks. We went to a little market where he bought me a pre-mixed, margarita-type drink in a little bottle, which was something you couldn't buy in Oregon at that time. You could only buy beer and wine in a little market. I remember thinking it was kind of cool. We got back to the room and he opened the little bottle for me. I took a drink. It didn't taste good. He encouraged me to take a few more swigs, claiming it would taste better the more I drank. Then he told me to change into my nightie. *That's at least better than getting naked.*

He raped me that night. I didn't resist and it was over very quickly. Even if there isn't a struggle, it is still rape, especially when there is financial and emotional dependence on the offender.

Do you realize rape can occur without a struggle? Without a physical altercation?

The third night, he took me out to a fancy dinner. He ordered wine and let me have sips of it when no one was looking. We had a secret no one else knew about. I was seriously thinking that this might work out. I would get a car and have a secret apartment. I was feeling a bit like a princess. My mind entertaining that this was going to be a loving relationship – a special one, a unique one. I was romanticizing it. It is horrid to think about how distorted my thinking was.

Then, almost as soon as I thought it, my bubble got popped. I went from feeling special to thinking, *I can't believe I almost fell for this crap.* What changed? He flirted with the waitress, totally obviously, and was oblivious to me, his new lover. He was not loving. He was not loyal. I was just another notch in his belt, another secret. I didn't want sex without love, but that's what this relationship would be for me.

He even had the audacity to ask me if I thought the busboy was cute. He whispered to me what he thought was a "great" idea. He would get a room for me and the busboy, and he and the waitress would use the room we already had rented.

I said, "Absolutely not!" This was not the sweet little romance I was imagining. I wanted something exclusive. That's what I thought gave sex any meaning – exclusivity. That's how sex became love. Otherwise, it was just sex.

I knew then and there that when we were back home, I was ending this short-lived affair. That last night, as he was raping me, I remember looking at the ceiling thinking, *if he was any good at this, it might be worth it to have this little secret and get a new car.* Again horrid, such distorted thinking for a 15-year-old girl to have. That would be the last time he ever climbed on top of me.

Can you look back on your young adult life and see how some of your thinking and choices were so mislead?

Can you see how some of your choices gave you an illusion of control?

The Last Time

I DECIDED TO tell Dad my decision the next time we were alone. I wasn't sure how I was going to tell him though and when that would be. I figured it would probably get physical, but I was scared, excited and determined. The five years of mental and sexual abuse were going to be over. At the time, we were living in one of the many homes my dad had built. This house was one of the few tri-levels. Even after 40 years I still remember the address.

Less than two days after I had made my decision and we were back home, Dad and I were alone together. He planned it. *Little did he know what I had planned.* It was a rare non- rainy day in the Pacific NW towards the end of winter. When I got off the school bus in our cul-de-sac, I noticed one of our cars was gone. This was a hopeful sight for me because it could mean no parents were home.

Since we had our own business, I was rarely home alone. Mom was usually home, but not that day. That day, my mom had gone into the office and my dad had stayed home. He opened the front door for me. This was even rarer than a sunny winter day and was creepy on top of it. My heart leaped in my chest as a rush of adrenaline was released in my body. *Today was the day the abuse would end* was firmly planted in my mind, and my dad was about to find out. What I didn't know is what it would cost me.

He teasingly said, "How about some afternoon delight?"

I said, "No, it's not going to happen."

As I moved past him in the entryway.

He said, "Oh, come on."

He started walking towards me. I started walking away. He gently took a hold of my arm like a lover and began to pull me in for a kiss. I spun my way out of the embrace and jumped down the five stairs into the family room. He was acting all coy, walking down the stairs, thinking I was playing hard to get. Inside, I was so happy to know there was about to be a fight, which was why I purposely moved into the family room. I kept walking away from him until we were in an area more conducive to a struggle.

He was so much bigger than me. He was a strong man. He was physically fit at this time in his life and I was ready to be knocked out cold. So what…I would do whatever it took, because this was the end of it. He grabbed my arm again with a firmer grip so I wouldn't be able to spin out of it. He was done playing. I tried to get away from this even stronger grip on my arm, but not a chance. This 15-year-old girl didn't have the physical ability to take on this 35-year-old man.

We began struggling and he forced me to the floor. He had me pinned. He was straddling me, and his hands had both my hands pinned above my head. As he tilted his head to the right and leaned down to kiss me, I grabbed a handful of hair. I grabbed as much hair as I could as tightly as I could. I knew this was my only leverage. This was my only shot. He was not going to be able to get out of the grip I had on his hair without losing a big hunk of it. And my dad was proud of his hair. He told me to let go.

"No," I said. "You let me up."

This went back and forth a couple of times with both of us raising our voices. His firm daddy voice and a look that was supposed to scare the little girl into obedience wasn't successful. *Not this time buster!* Finally, he moved off me and I kept my handful of his hair and we stood up together. I felt like I had so much power, gripping his hair in my hand. He couldn't even stand upright because I was shorter than him. I still love that vision. It's like a David and Goliath moment to me.

That's when I told him, with as much venom, power and strength as I could bring to my voice, as I looked him in the eyes in his hunched over position with my fingers still gripping his hair as tightly as I could:

"You will never touch me again. The only way you will ever have sex with me again is if I am unconscious. You would have to knock me out and that will leave a bruise or mark on my body that Mom will see, and then she will know!"

I shoved his head away from me as I let go of his hair and boldly walked back up the five stairs into the entry, turned to the left, walked up the 12 stairs to my bedroom and shut the door.

How did your sexual abuse end?

Was there a confrontation?

Did your predator move or were you able to distance yourself from him or her?

Did your predator move onto another victim because you were no longer a child?

Part 2

IMPACT HAPPENS

(the strong effect or influence that something has on a situation or person so that the actions they take and the choices they make are now not healthy because of it)

Abuse Leads to Abuse

THE FIRST TIME I ever sexually abused someone was within a year of having been abused myself. I was 11. It was the children of my mom's friends, a brother and sister, who had come to stay the night. Basically, I was trying to figure out how to process what had happened to me. My dad said that I should have liked it and there might be something wrong with me. I wanted to see how other kids around my age would respond. I still didn't like it. I didn't want anything to do with it. They didn't seem to like it, either.

About a year later, I sexually abused two boys who I was babysitting. I didn't plan it. The boys had stumbled across their parents' private stash of pornography. Some people wouldn't even say what happened was sexual abuse, more like children playing and natural curiosity. I have come to know that any form of secrets related to sex is abuse when it involves minors. It doesn't have to be physical. It can be mental and emotional. It doesn't have to be an adult to a child. It can be a child to a child. When a person's sexuality is involved, especially for young children, distortion occurs. I don't know where these boys are right now in their adult lives, but if they are addicted to porn or have trouble with loving, intimate relationships, this incident could be the seed that started it.

There are two other incidences that took place with minors when I was not a minor that I also consider to be sexual abuse. Others may disagree, but they would be romanticizing it like Hollywood movies often do. There is nothing romantic about abusing a minor.

Were you abused by another child?

Do you feel like your abuse lead you to abuse someone?

Becoming a Call Girl

AFTER PUTTING AN end to the abuse by my dad, which happened halfway through my freshman year of high school, I started abusing myself. At the time I would have never thought of it that way. In my mind, I thought I was choosing to live the way I wanted to live – partying, getting drunk, screwing around. But hindsight reveals something darker was prompting those activities. I was just trying to run and hide from all the horrible feelings incest had created.

Sex became my tool. It gave me a feeling of control and power. It was my body and I could use it anyway I wanted. There was that "illusion of choice" again. You really aren't in a place of choosing when you don't have all the correct information or when your wounds are directing you. Taking care of your body and mind is what a person, given the right foundation of the value of their body and mind, would do. Emotionally healthy people wouldn't harm their own body, abusing it with alcohol, drugs and sex. But I can guarantee no one could have convinced me of that back then. I was a rebel and proud of it.

Have you ever thought about how abusing substances or sex might stem from your abuse?

During Christmas break in my first year of college, I went to stay with family friends for a few days. I would be flying to meet my folks in Germany, and since that was a couple of days into my break and my mom didn't want me to feel like I was alone over the holidays, she arranged for me to spend time with our long-time family friends. Remember the family friends my dad had told me those secrets about? The threesome they had and the wife taking the virginity of my cousin, who was 13 at the time and she was almost 30? *Those* family friends.

They let me have a couple of beers with dinner. I was 18 and the drinking age in Oregon is 21. As you already know, I was already into alcohol. After dinner the husband and I went on a snowmobile ride to a frozen pond. We got stoned. We sat down on the frozen pond looking up at the winter night sky. It was gorgeous. The multitude of twinkling stars were amazing.

We started talking about my future and the things I could do. I was young and beautiful. He told me that he knew men, friends of his, who would pay $400 or $500 to have sex with me, maybe more. He could set it up. These wouldn't be strangers; I would be safe. They would treat me right. They would *adore* me. Looking up at the expansive sky and all those stars (while high), I felt like the world was my oyster. I could use my body to make me rich.

I said, "Yes, call me when I get back from Germany and let's get started right away."

I wanted to be wined and dined and made to feel like a princess…and make money at the same time.

Do you even realize how sad that story is? Do you realize how many girls end up in the sex industry because they were abused? I was willing to sell my own body. I was willing to use my body in a way that it wasn't meant to be used. Why? Because I had been groomed and trained to see my body that way. In my twisted thinking, I actually believed it was a healthy option to choose. Was it really my choice? I would have argued with you that it was my choice, but several different visits to different counselors as an adult would show me that wasn't the case.

Obviously, it wasn't a healthy choice. It wasn't even a true choice at all. What we experience determines the choices we make. We don't know any better.

I never did become a call girl. For some reason the husband never called me after Christmas break to make the arrangements.

Have you been divinely protected from taking action on a bad choice?

Marrying a Narcissist

BACK AT THE University of Oregon, I continued my destructive path, drinking, doing drugs and having sex. I had several black outs and several regrets; several one-night stands and a couple of boyfriends. I totaled two vehicles while drinking and driving. There are so many more stories I could tell you about how I wasn't making the right choices. There's the time I almost died in the middle of a blackout while driving, the time I took acid and almost lost my mind, the time I was drinking with a homeless person on the streets of Portland, or the time a boyfriend and I got stabbed by a person we gave a ride to who tried to steal my boyfriend's car. All this and much more happened in my two short years of college. After that, I dropped out.

I met my wasband (he "was" my husband) in June of 1983. It's an interesting story, but for another time. We got serious quickly. Our third date was a three-day getaway to Victoria, British Columbia. He wined and dined me and spent a lot of money. I would later find out that is typical of a high-functioning narcissist. Extravagant gifts are given early on to woo in their unsuspecting victims. It's called "love bombing."

I always told my serious relationships about the incest. I didn't want to have any secrets. I also shared some of my stupid and shameful sexual encounters. Maybe I was looking for sympathy, maybe even pity or wanting to know if they could love me despite being damaged goods. My wasband romanticized it, not the incest, but the other things. He wanted to hear more about them and know the details. He thought that it sounded exciting.

I had never met anyone who responded that way to what I felt so ashamed about. It made me feel better about myself – special, unique, desirable. It's why there are things like Playboy, Penthouse and the whole pornography industry: they take advantage of distorted femininity. He romanticized my screwed up, self-abusive sex life. He wanted to know everything about me. I found it very charming. He was idolizing me and my past. It's all part of love bombing, which is also referred to as the idolization stage that is typical of a narcissist.

What I think was so intoxicating about this was that I finally felt like I could accept myself. His proclamations of unconditional love made me feel adored and I began to feel worthy and valuable. I felt whole, finally able to love myself. He was continually speaking about how special I was, how I was the best thing that ever happened to him and how lucky he was. He wanted to know everything about me. Later, however, he would be using everything he learned against me and to control me.

I was living in an apartment with my two girlfriends when we met. He was charming enough to them, but when we were alone, he would say things like, "I think they are really shallow. I'm not sure they're good for you." Seeding my mind with doubt, his goal was for me to move out and live with him.

My friends tried to warn me. They told me he was being way to possessive. "He's too controlling." I tried to explain to them that he was a great guy, how he was not very trusting until he really knew you, how he had been really hurt in his childhood, and that he needed me. I was already sucked in by how he adored me. Shortly into the relationship, I had dumped all my friends and it was just him and me. Isolation from others is another technique used by a narcissist.

Are you familiar with the term narcissist?

Do you have any experiences with a narcissist?

Drinking is the Problem

WE DATED FOR several months, lived together for two years and then got married in 1986. We had "good drunk" times in the beginning, and then "bad drunk" times started happening. His jealousy and narcissism were the cause of the bad drunk times. All the things he wanted to know about my past were now used against me. I thought drinking was the problem. Eliminate drinking, no more problem, right? Short term it worked, but not long term because drinking was only a part of the problem.

Two years into our marriage (when I was 25), while we were in a fight one drunk night, we walked in the front door of our house and I went straight for the Yellow Pages. Yes, the Yellow Pages! This was long before the Internet and smartphones. I was flipping frantically through it by the time he walked in the door.

He yelled, "What are you doing?"

I yelled back, "I am calling Alcoholics Anonymous!"

He left the kitchen area in disbelief and disgust. I found the number for the local AA program. I dialed it and a man answered. Talking with a man about this wasn't good for me because of my wasband's jealousy, but I had no choice. I wanted help. I started crying and stuttered out the words, "I…I think I have a drinking problem."

He said something about being glad I had called in, and, "Can I get your number so a lady can call you back and you'll be able to talk more comfortably?" *Absolutely!* I was impressed that he seemed to understand my position without me saying anything at all. How did he know my wasband was a jealous narcissist? I gave him my number and hung up.

Wasband came back to the kitchen to find out what was going on. I told him a lady from AA was going to be calling me back. I made myself a stiff drink, since this was going to be the end of my drinking. The phone rang. I answered. It was a lady named Dana. I immediately started crying, stuttering and trying to spit out again that I think I have a drinking problem.

She asked me, "What are you drinking now?"

Wow! You people really do get me. I was super impressed she would know that I was drinking *while* confessing to having a drinking problem. She invited me to an AA meeting. There was a women's meeting coming up Saturday at 3 p.m. She said she would call tomorrow and gave me directions.

I drank for the rest of the night, finishing all the vodka we had. The next day was terrible; I had the worst hangover. By the time the meeting rolled around, I still had the dry heaves. It was horrible and there was no way I could go to the meeting. Dana invited me to the next one, which was a mixed meeting with men and women. I told her I could only go to a women's meeting because of my wasband's jealousy. That wouldn't be until Thursday.

I said, "I'll be there."

Later, she told me she didn't believe I'd actually show up. Most alcoholics who don't get to a meeting right away keep on drinking until it gets worse. She thought I was another alcoholic who was going to stay stuck, but that wasn't the case this time. She became my sponsor.

My first AA meeting changed my life. I felt like I was home. People welcomed me and did not judge. For the first time in my life I felt known, like I didn't need to hide anymore. These were my people and they got me from Step 1. We admitted "we were powerless over alcohol – that our lives had become unmanageable." I already and very clearly knew that was true for me. It was the reason I was there. That was why I made the call. Soon, I would realize that kind of honesty and the admission of powerlessness was life-changing. It would lead me to release my shame.

Step 2 showed me where I could find power in my powerlessness. We "came to believe that a power greater than ourselves could restore us to sanity." *You mean God?* I did believe there was something more to this world, that there was a Creator. It just made sense to me. What kind of sense is it that something crawled out of the water, learned to breathe, developed legs, lost its tail, and learned to walk upright? It takes more faith to believe in evolution than creation.

The extraordinary uniqueness in the world disproves evolution. Evolution is just not probable. Take a look at one animal species: there are over 9000 types of birds! How did that come about from one Big Bang? Even Darwin couldn't explain why traits varied within a species, or how they were passed on from generation to generation. Science has mistakenly taken his hypothesis for fact.

The God who I believed in before learning about Step 2 created everything, but I thought He, She or It was not involved in helping individuals. It was all based on the "luck of the draw" and what we did personally to help ourselves. I felt like God was up in the heavens somewhere, looking down on us like a bunch of ants, watching us for His entertainment. If you happened to read the right book or meet the right person so you could get more out of this life, then He was like, "Oh, yippy...good for them." And if not... then, "Too bad, so sad." Basically, I believed life is what you made it, and good luck with making the best of it. There is actually a name for this kind of belief: it's called Deism. My dad was an atheist. I considered my mom to be a closet Catholic, basically God was not spoken about, so I was left to my own conclusion.

AA was telling me that my whole idea of God hanging out up there, watching us from above and having a good laugh at us or feeling sorry for us wasn't true. So, my whole concept of God was wrong all this time?

Learning that God would personally help me changed *everything*. I had a power Who I could call on! He cared about me enough to empower me to do what I couldn't do before (alone). I was elated. I was (what AA refers to as) "on a pink cloud." It was the wonderful new world of sobriety, along with a personal higher power. I loved knowing there was a power I could tap into.

Within the first few meetings of sitting and listening to ladies share their stories of how alcohol had impacted their lives and why they drank, a new truth hit me. I had been using alcohol to deal with all the mixed-up feelings from my dad sexually abusing me. I shared my story in the group. The feelings started coming back and I was processing them. They were feelings and memories I had buried deep. I began to recognize how my partying and sexual promiscuity were not by choice…but by conditioning.

Dana and I would talk about whether I was going to say something to my mom, or my dad, or both. I felt like I didn't necessarily need to say anything to my mom, but I did want an apology from my dad. He needed to acknowledge that what he did to me was wrong, how it had messed me up and that he was sorry.

Have you used alcohol or drugs to deal with emotional hurts?

Have you felt that since the abuse is done and over, what would there be to heal from?

Can you see how you could have current behaviors that may be more about conditioning than choice?

Mom Knows

A FEW MONTHS into my sobriety, I invited my mom to lunch. We were already seated at the I-Hop restaurant in Gresham, Oregon on Stark Street. She sat on the bench seat and I was in the chair directly across from her. It was a table for four. I can still picture the scene. Then, surprisingly, in walked my dad. He went to slide into the bench and my mom slid over, so now I was sitting directly across from him. I tried not to show my disappointment.

He started in right away with, "How's the not drinking going?"

I told them about the pink cloud and how happy I was, and how sobriety could bring up past issues that needed to be worked through. I wanted to drop a little hint to my dad that we should probably talk sometime separately.

He said, "Like what?"

*You have got to be kidding me? Like what? You know what, you jerk...*I wanted to reach over the table and slap him across the face.

Instead, I said very calmly with my heart racing in my chest, "Just different stuff that happened when I was growing up. Like how you have treated me, how you treated mom, just stuff."

He shrugged it off and said, "I have something funny to show you guys."

He pulled out his wallet and unfolded a piece of a magazine. It was a little cartoon, showing a couple sitting across a desk from a psychiatrist. The caption says, "Just slap the bitch." I was so offended, and it got worse. Printed in the corner I saw that the page was from Hustler magazine, which is a horribly raunchy porn magazine. I just pushed it back across the table to him and again thought, *what a stupid jerk. Is he trying to push me to say something?* I didn't want to say something in front of my mom. I wanted to talk to him privately. The whole thing had been a secret anyway; I could talk to him in secret again. We could keep it a secret. I just wanted an apology; It wasn't about breaking up my parents.

Predators try to keep control over their victims, which is why my dad had showed up uninvited to lunch. My dad was trying to keep me quiet. Showing me a woman being slapped because she's not staying "in her place" in a cartoon from a magazine was a calculated strategy. It confirmed the only value a woman has according to him. He was trying to keep his power. He, like my wasband, was a sexual narcissist.

After lunch we all left in our separate cars. I headed home. As my mom headed to her car, my dad said to her, "I want you to stay away from Jeanette. She's dangerous."

This was another attempt at trying to maintain control. My mom told me that she was thinking, *what are you talking about?* and got in her car.

Later that afternoon, I got a call from my mom asking if she could come over. It sounded like she may have been crying.

I said, "Sure" and we hung up.

I called my AA sponsor, told her what happened at lunch and that my mom was on her way over. We both felt like we knew what was about to happen. The secret would not be a secret anymore. Dana gave me a pep talk and we prayed together. God was there to help me and give me the words. I believed and trusted in that.

It took my mom less than 20 minutes to get to my house. She knocked on the door. I opened it. She stood there and started to cry while she choked out the words, "Just tell me…did he?"

She couldn't even finish the question. I slowly, with barely any movement, nodded my head yes. She dropped her head into her hands as if to keep it from falling to the ground. I stepped out to her, put my arm around her shoulder and guided her inside. We embraced, cried and held each other in the entryway. Years of baggage was going to begin to be unpacked.

After several minutes of our emotions pouring out, I led her to the kitchen table. We sat down. I put the kettle on for tea. She told me how sorry she was and how she didn't know. She was still sobbing. Looking back, she told me there was a time when she had suspected something; a night when he came home drunk and she found him sitting on the edge of my bed rubbing my back while I was sleeping.

She asked him, "What are you doing?"

He said, "Just loving our daughter."

She told him to get to bed and pointed to their room. This was before the actual abuse. I was around eight years old.

I told her that I forgive her and that I know that if she knew, she would have left him. She would have protected me.

She asked, "Why didn't you tell me?"

"I thought you'd go back to Germany, and I didn't want to do that." I explained to her that just knowing she would have left him if I told her gave me a huge sense of security and strength.

Did you ever tell your mom or dad about the abuse?

Why or why not?

Did they believe you?

Mom Has a Secret

THE TEA KETTLE whistled. I sat back down with our cups of tea and she said to me very seriously, "I have something to tell you."

My first thought was full of hope. I was thinking she was going to tell me that my dad wasn't really my dad after all. Ha! Maybe Peter, a boy she had liked in Germany who I had heard about, was my real dad. I don't know where this thought came from…wishful thinking, I guess. What she actually told me though was about my dead uncle, Phil.

My Uncle Phil had drowned in a boating accident with my dad in the Strait of Juan de Fuca and the body was never found. We (my mom, me and Phil's wife and four kids) had all thought that he wasn't actually dead. We had all suspected that the brothers were defrauding the life insurance company. That's the kind of people they were. What changed

Joy Restored

my mind, though, was when my cousin Renee showed up at our front door.

She was the female version of my uncle. She looked so much like her dad. When my dad opened the door, I was coming down the stairs into the entryway. I saw him collapse with emotion to the floor, holding his head and crying. It was so extreme and expressive. His crumbling and crying seeing the daughter of the man he had not kept safe on his boat and now was dead. What had he done? That was when I felt certain Uncle Phil was dead. There was no way someone could respond so passionately if it was all a lie. I was purposely there to see my dad's response. Before that I had been watching him closely for signs of deception. That day, though, I thought I knew the truth. *Uncle Phil was dead.*

In fact, my mom told me that *wasn't* the case; Uncle Phil *wasn't* dead. It was insurance fraud to get the money after all. She hadn't been part of the plan, although Uncle Mitch (the other brother) and his wife had been. They knew that my mom wouldn't go along with it. They also knew they could tell her afterwards and she wouldn't rat them out. She found out the same way my grandma, his mom, found out.

My Uncle Mitch bought a yacht with some of the insurance money and was down in Florida. My dad, mom and grandma all flew down for a visit. There they all were, sitting anchored out on the yacht, with a little boat rowing towards them. Guess who was in it? It turned out to be Uncle Phil! Can you even imagine his mother's response? They are lucky she didn't have a heart attack. She was 74 years old!

I was blown away about how my dad was such a good actor. My mom told me not to tell anyone or they might do something to "silence" us. The two older brothers were scary that way. They had stories. In their younger years, they had robbed a couple of Safeway stores at gunpoint. Phil and Mitch were about 14 years older than my dad. My dad was one of those trailer babies, or stragglers, or whatever it is you call the unexpected ones born after you've had kids years earlier. That was another thing my wasband had in common with my dad. His mom thought that she had the flu but she was pregnant.

Do you think your family has other secrets besides incest?

Do you know what they are?

I'll Kill Him

MY MOM WENT back home that day with the intent to kill my dad. She got out one of his many guns, a little revolver, sat down on the couch and waited for him to walk through the door. She imagined confronting him while aiming the gun at his chest and then pulling the trigger. When she left my home, I did not know about her deadly intentions. I wouldn't have let her go if I had. On her way out, she told me that she didn't know what she was going to do – probably just go to bed and fall into an exhausted sleep, and I believed her.

My dad had been on pretty good behavior for a couple of years – not staying out late anymore, not getting drunk, not carousing, but coming home in the evenings instead. That night, though, he stayed out past 10 p.m. My mom had fallen asleep on the couch with the gun under the pillow. She woke up when he came in, but pretended to be asleep. He sat down on a nearby chair and turned on the news. She watched him with an eye slightly open, thinking about what a horrible thing he had done, what a horrible man he was; an evil man. He deserved to be shot, but as she lay there, she realized if she shot him, *she would be doing a horrible thing too*. She would go to jail and leave me behind dealing with one, great big emotional mess.

Instead, she made another plan. She would get up early, go to her friend's house and call him from there, telling him to get out of the house, they were getting a divorce and that she knew what he had done to their little girl. She would tell him that there was nothing to talk about and he needed to get out of the house.

It Doesn't Have to be This Way

MY DAD WOUND up calling me crying, asking if we could talk. Of course, we could talk. That's all I wanted in the first place after all, to talk to him and tell him how what he had done really messed me up by distorting my view of love, sex and femininity, which are the very foundation of relationships. He needed to know it was a horrible thing for him to do. I just wanted his acknowledgment of that. I just wanted him to admit it was wrong; that he was wrong.

Even so, I was scared to have him come over to my house. I didn't know what he was going to do. I didn't know if he'd try to hurt me in some way. I had just turned his world upside down. Maybe he was going to kill me? He had faked my uncle's death, so maybe he knew of a way to kill me and not get caught. I said we could meet in the parking lot at the strip mall near my house. He could get in my car and we could talk. I definitely wasn't going to get in his car and have him drive off with me. He agreed, and we met that afternoon.

He got in my car, didn't even look at me. He sat as close to the door as he could with his head in his hands and sobbed. I didn't say a word. I let him cry. I knew what a good actor he was, figuring it was all a show. When he finally looked at me, I think he was surprised by my straight-faced lack of compassion. He didn't know I knew that Uncle Phil wasn't dead. The first words out of his mouth took me by surprise. I don't know what I was expecting. I knew what I wanted though; I wanted an apology. I was prepared to accept one and forgive him.

But he said, through fake tears and red swollen eyes, "How could you hate your mom so much?"

I was dumbfounded...what did this have to do with hating my mom? Was he crazy?

No, he wasn't crazy. He was just a pro at manipulating. It was a masterful art he had perfected. It's also known as gaslighting. It's what narcissists do to not be accountable for their own bad behavior. He wanted *me* to feel guilty for what was happening between them. He still wasn't going to take any responsibility for it.

I adamantly said, "I don't hate my mom and I don't hate you. I forgive you. I know that things happened to you when you were a child by your older brothers or you wouldn't have done it to me."

Defensibly he said, "Nothing happened to me as a child."

I said, "Yes, it did. A person doesn't do what you did to me without it having been done to them. It's a learned behavior, not a natural one." I told him, "I never wanted to tell mom. I wanted to talk to *you* in private, but you pushed me into dropping a little hint at the restaurant by having that horrible cartoon clipping from that smutty magazine. You weren't even supposed to be there. I wasn't going to tell her a thing. I was planning on talking to you alone to get an apology. I was surprised by mom's phone call and her asking if she could come over. I thought she had put two and two together. I didn't know that you had told her to stay away from me. That I was dangerous!? That was pretty stupid on your part. When I opened the door all she asked me was, 'Did he?'"

I paused for a moment to see if he had anything to say. He didn't. His mind was probably still spinning with how he could fix all of this and get it back under control.

I said, "We can go to counseling together. I am open to that."

He wasn't. He got out of the car, looked at me one more time, and said almost the same thing he said when he got in: "How could you hate us so much?"

Isn't that just like a narcissist? Never taking responsibility and twisting things in order to live in their delusion...

That was pretty much the last time I would ever talk to my dad. My mom did divorce him and he ran off to Mexico.

Were you able to confront your abuser?

Did it go the way you thought it would?

What were the results?

It's an Internal Affair

THERE WERE SO many different things that stood out during my early healing process. One of the foundational breakthroughs was when Cheryl, a counselor, was trying to explain to me how it wasn't my fault, how I was taking on a responsibility that wasn't mine. I just couldn't see it. Maybe at ten years old it wasn't my fault, but at 15…it was. And now at 24, I was not going to let my 15-year-old self off the hook. *I went to CA with my dad. I considered having a secret relationship with him to get a car and whatever else I could get out of it. I was responsible and I was in control.* That's all there was to it. There was nothing that could convince me otherwise, which slams a door on any further healing of sexual abuse. If you can't let yourself realize that you were a victim, you can't get to those feelings of vulnerability you had as a child so the feelings can be processed and released. You will remain stuck.

In order for me to change my mind, God set up a surprise meeting for me with my dad. Now that I had a better understanding of God working in my life, I gave Him credit for these kinds of "coincidental" events that happened and allowed further healing. I knew healing was what He wanted for me; complete healing, to be Innocent Again. I called these divinely coordinated events "Godincidences."

At the time, I was working at Fairview Management, which was the business where my folks had their bookkeeping and taxes done. When I was leaving work, my dad was coming in. We passed each other on the side of the building – me going to the parking lot, him coming from the parking lot to the front door. It had been in the parking lot at the strip mall where I had last seen or heard from him. In the meantime, I had imagined running into him and getting a chance to give him a piece of my mind. I wanted to tell him how what he had done really messed me up. As we were walking towards each other, and then past each other, I couldn't say a word. It was like my mouth was slammed shut. It wouldn't open. I couldn't speak.

After we were past each other, he turned around and said, "Hi." I looked over my shoulder, still walking away, and barely got "hi" out of my mouth.

I got in my car and started shaking uncontrollably. My hands gripped the steering wheel as I tried

Joy Restored

to calm myself and get grounded. Fear was spreading through my whole body. I was really starting to freak out.

I lifted my eyes and looked at myself in the rearview mirror. God revealed to me, in an instant, the reality of my 15-year-old self; that 15-year-old, distorted girl who I wanted to think was so in charge and therefore responsible for what happened to her. There was no possible way that could be true. The 24-year-old me couldn't even say anything to that man right now, having just been given the opportunity. How in the world could I even think my 15-year-old self-had any control? She was groomed, manipulated and controlled. She was doing the best she could in that situation. Just because I put an end to it after the trip to CA, it didn't mean I was responsible for it. It didn't mean I had chosen it.

After that breakthrough realization, I could finally release responsibility for the incest. I could start processing through the other lies and faulty beliefs I held on to. My patterns of wrong thinking were invasive. I became a sponge, soaking up the right way of thinking. In learning, there was a lot of unlearning that had to happen.

Books full of wisdom and mindset shifts were my new friends. I went to weekend seminars specifically designed to dig deep into how past hurts had a hold on me in ways I didn't fully understand or recognize.

There were step-by-step processes, games, exercises and journaling all meant to bring out any false beliefs that were holding me back. There were some amazing, miraculous mental and emotional healings during that time period, including healing with my mom.

Have you sought out any professional help?

Do you believe that professional counseling can help?

Drinking's Not the Only Problem

I DIDN'T SUSPECT anything. He didn't appear to be a womanizer like my dad. I didn't think he saw women as sex objects. It's not the way he behaved in public, he didn't gawk at them or try and flirt with them, but unbeknownst to me he had a secret life of pornography, strip joints and the occasional prostitute.

Our sex life was very intense in the beginning. He seemed to be so tuned into how I was feeling, wanting to know exactly what I wanted. He wanted to be the best lover I ever had. That is what a sexual narcissist does. They don't do it for you though; they do it for the attention to be on *them* and how great *they* are. It's another form of manipulation and control.

After several years of marriage our sex life started to seem mechanical. I started feeling used more than loved and tried to talk to him about it. That's when

I learned of his pornography addiction. He wanted me to get involved in it. He said that would help our sex life. I didn't like it. Porn made me feel insecure and jealous, as it does for most women. I felt like he wanted the woman on the screen or the picture in the magazine more than me.

We'd end up in a big fight, with me crying saying that he didn't love me. He told me it wasn't about him wanting another woman, but to add spice to our lives. Then like any good manipulative, controlling person does, he wore me down. He came at it from different angles, saying things like:

"If you loved me, you would want to do what makes me happy."

"If you cared about our relationship, you would do things to prove it."

"You only care about yourself and aren't concerned for my feelings."

I began to question my perception of sex and love making. Since I was sexually abused as a child, maybe I was all wrong?

By this time, I had become isolated again and didn't have anyone to talk to about it. I had long since quit going to AA meetings. That had only lasted a few months, because remember, a narcissist needs to isolate you. If he didn't need them, he convinced me I didn't need them either. Feelings of shame came back because I thought I wasn't woman enough to keep my husband satisfied. I caved. I started participating with pornography.

As the years went by, his sex addiction grew like addictions are prone to do. Now it wasn't just pornography. Next came phone sex, which led to other deviant behaviors involving other people face to face. All the while, I was going along with these things, trying to get a feeling of love, and in my distorted view of sex and love, sometimes even feeling loved. No one knew. I never talked to anyone about it. Once my wasband knew how much I loved him because of what I was willing to do for him, it could all stop, right?

But it wasn't stopping. It was getting worse. I wasn't feeling loved anymore; I was feeling used. "Spicing up our marriage" like he said it would was a lie. It was destroying our marriage…destroying me. When would it ever end? It was like watching a monster grow, getting out of control. Being sexually and emotionally abused by my wasband, I'd lost myself. I didn't know who I was, what I liked or what I wanted anymore. All my focus was on trying to please him and I lost myself. It was like hanging by a thread, just coping, barely hanging on.

Do you feel like you are easily manipulated and controlled because of being abused as a child?

Did you do things you didn't want to do to feel loved?

Have you found yourself in abusive relationships?

Off and On the Wagon

WE HAD SOBER years and drunk years, and through them all was the craziness and gaslighting that accompanies a narcissist. I was a shell of a person, merely a puppet. In our third alcoholic relapse, I ended up being bold enough to tell him I would no longer participate with pornography or any of the other deviant sexual behaviors. He punched a hole in the wall right next to my face.

After 13 years of marriage, I had become suicidal. I started thinking that our kids (1-year-old boy, 4-year-old girl) and my wasband would be better off without me. He made it very clear he loved them more than me; he told me so. "I would leave you if it wasn't for the kids."

I sought out counseling; I needed help. The nearest counselor who our insurance covered was a man. This time, I decided I was not going to appease my wasband and get a woman counselor. Taking care of myself was the priority.

The first order of business with the therapist was to get me on antidepressants, which I didn't want to take. There I was…someone who used alcohol and pot on and off through the years to alter my mental state and deal with the emotional and sexual abuse, yet was reluctant to take medication. Why wouldn't I want to take something designed to help me, not hurt me? I asked him if antidepressants would change my personality. He gave me a great explanation about how the drinking, pot and emotional stresses had caused damage to the chemical balance in my brain. He confronted my hesitation with the truth. "You are already out of balance and not your real self anymore. You probably haven't been that person for a long time." (Boy, did he have that right!) I decided to give the medication a try, which meant no more alcohol again. I threatened my wasband with leaving with the kids if he didn't stop drinking. So once again, in 2001, we were both on the wagon.

Have you used substances like alcohol or drugs to emotionally cope?

Have you used activities like shopping or gambling to distract yourself from your hurts?

Sober Again

THIS TIME AROUND I involved God more. There was a nearby church I started attending regularly. I went to the women's Bible study, which, of all things, was led by the Pastor (a man). Now I had my second healthy male authority figure in my life (the first one being my counselor). I desperately needed healthy, safe male figures in my life who I could respect and trust. I felt like it was God's way of letting me see there were good men in the world; men who could be trusted. Pastor Snavely was so helpful with that. Even now I still remember some of the great biblical truths I learned from him. It was another step towards self-care.

I also did a program called *The Bondage Breaker* by Neil T. Anderson. I spent 10.5 hours with two lady pastors, going over every situation that came to mind where darkness, lies, distorted thinking and wrong behaviors could have entered into my life. It was intense and definitely broke unhealthy patterns. These were even more steps in the right direction of self-care.

I believe that those steps and getting to know God better are what kept me sober when my wasband started drinking again.

Replaced and Discarded

NOW THAT I was no longer feeding his narcissism because I was doing things he didn't approve of (having a male counselor, threatening to take the kids if he didn't stop drinking, wasn't remaining isolated), he started looking elsewhere to feed his narcissism. It just so happened that a young, attractive woman got hired at his work to be his assistant. Thus began his discarding of me and his obsession with her.

We moved to Sauvie Island in 2004. We had a mini farm with several kinds of farm animals. I was loving life and enjoying homeschooling the kids. My wasband and I were no longer having sexual relations, but I figured it was just a dry season in our lives. The roommate type of relationship we were having was actually enjoyable. He wasn't trying to control me as much anymore. I felt a new sense of freedom. Then came the fateful day, after about a year on the island, when my wasband came home from work smelling like alcohol.

He walked through the door and greeted our dog, our beautiful great big Greater Swiss/Bernese Mountain dog mix named Blue (he had one blue eye). I squatted down with him to join in the petting and thought I smelled alcohol. *That can't be.* I ignored it. He continued loving on Blue, who of course was soaking it all in. I smelled the alcohol again and felt like I should say something.

Fear started welling up inside of me. This couldn't be. He couldn't be drinking. If he was drinking, he didn't love me. He didn't care about me. I felt like I was disconnecting from myself, like I was about to float out of my body. I had to say something or I would float away. I lightly, jokingly made a comment while rubbing on Blue, trying to keep this realization at bay.

"I smell alcohol." I said it with the tone like, *isn't that just the strangest thing?*

He answered like it was a common occurrence, like *of course, why wouldn't I smell it.*

"I had some beers at work. One of our vendors dropped off a six pack and I drank a few."

I was too shocked to even say anything. I went right back into being a victim.

The next couple of nights, he came home after work smelling of alcohol. He was all happy and

Joy Restored

playing with the kids. With each evening, I started to feel like my life was unraveling before my eyes. I told him that if he was going to keep on drinking, he needed to tell the kids he was drinking. I wanted them to know that this "new" dad who comes home all happy was not what it looked like. We had told our kids about our drinking DNA and why we didn't drink. We explained how they would need to be careful with alcohol, since addiction problems with it run in the family.

I figured he would rather stop drinking than tell the kids he was drinking, but sadly, no. With this current buzz on, he was like, "Hey kids, Daddy has a beer on his way home from work. It helps him relax after a hard day." He told them that he wouldn't be drinking at home and that it wasn't a big deal. That wasn't at all the correct perspective for them to have. I don't remember if I said anything as I watched my world fall apart.

This went on for a few months. I will not go into all the various ways I tried to fix it, but thankfully it did not involve me going back to any of our old dysfunctional patterns (like me drinking too). My heart was being broken piece by piece, one failed attempt after another, all the while, not knowing I had already been replaced.

A Hurtful Divorce

MY WHOLE WORLD was turned upside down. Twenty years to the day we signed divorce papers. I lost my life as I knew it. The kids were seven and ten at the time. I truly loved being a mom. I loved homeschooling them. Since the day they were born I had basically been with them 24/7. Our new little mini farm on the island was heavenly.

I was about to find out how cold-hearted my wasband was and how broken I was from the many years of emotional and sexual abuse. The divorce papers said I would have the kids all week and my wasband would have them on the weekends. This was so that I could continue homeschooling. I was so happy! I thought I was finally getting something I wanted from the divorce. I would have my kids the majority of the time!

But once again, my wasband had another plan in mind. He had a very expensive attorney and I was getting screwed. He wanted our kids in public school like the other woman's son was. I knew this, but he never brought it up while we negotiated the parenting plan. How could I still be so naïve to his manipulative ways?

After the papers were signed and I was back home, I got a call from him. He said to me that he knew what the divorce papers said, but that wasn't what was going to happen. He already had the kids registered to start school. I would have the kids on the weekend, and he would have them during the week. The alimony and child support payments would stay the same. And what did I say? I didn't say *anything*. I started crying. Crying! He started trying to console me. "It would be best for everyone. It is what the kids want" (he had already been convincing them of that).

Between my tears, I managed to get out an, "Okay," and told him I wanted to get off the phone. He had *played me* again. I didn't have the strength to fight and he knew it. He still controlled me.

Even three years after the divorce our interactions were still very emotionally hurtful. I was still heavily controlled and manipulated by him. Everything was done his way to keep the peace. Although I wasn't under the same roof as him anymore, he was still emotionally abusing me. I realized I needed to set boundaries. There were three issues that needed to be addressed: parenting schedule, picking up the kids and the kids' dogs.

As I tried to address these issues, he went into full attack mode. There was no winning with him. None of my boundaries were respected, and in the end, he caused the kids (11 and 14 years old) to be completely alienated from me. He was diabolical and evil – a true narcissist. Everyone was under his control and I had no strength to fight him. As I write this, it has been ten years since I have seen my kids. The emotional hurt from that is something I wouldn't wish on anyone. The only glimmer at the time was knowing at least I didn't have to deal with him anymore. I could begin to climb out from under the rock he kept me under.

Can you relate to being controlled as an adult by another adult?

Do you find it perplexing that an adult can have such power over another adult?

In order for that to happen, do you believe the oppressed adult must be distorted in some way previously, causing them to be pre-dispositioned to be controlled?

Pity Party

I ENDED UP mad at God because of the divorce and estrangement from my kids. Drinking, smoking pot and feeling sorry for myself was my response. I was diving deep into being a victim and how horrible life was. Whoever would listen got an earful about my woes, and I fed off their pity. *Poor Jeanette, she goes from being sexually abused by her dad to an emotionally and sexually abusive, narcissistic husband who manages to manipulate the situation and get her kids to not want to see her.* I had lost so much. It felt like everything. I had to get a job because I was no longer a stay-at-home homeschooling mom. I went from a 4038 square foot home on acreage to a 950 square foot apartment.

Several years were very difficult. When I decided to stop drinking, I gained over 60 lbs in a year. I was so broken, and even felt like if I were to see my kids, I wanted them to see how broken I was. A part of me felt like I couldn't get on with my life or enjoy my life.

If I did see my kids, I wanted them to feel sorry for me too. They should know being away from them tore me apart. I didn't want them to think I had wanted things this way.

Have you ever thrown yourself a pity party?

Have you ever done things so other people will feel sorry for you?

Part 3
INSPIRATION FOLLOWS
(To influence, move or guide by divine or supernatural inspiration.)

Healing is a Process

I AM SO excited to be to this section! Reliving and documenting my experiences in the previous two sections was daunting. That may have even been the case for you as you were reading it. If that's true, I am so proud of you for making it this far and so excited to be sharing this next section with you. Thank God I am done writing those sections and done living through that! I am so grateful.

Healing is definitely a process. It's not black and white, but gray and a different shade of gray for everyone. It is very personal. Expect you may have two steps forward and one step back…sometimes two or three back. The twists and turns along the path will be unique and yet similar to every traveler taking this journey. You are not alone. There are steps you can follow and signposts to guide you, yet the journey is yours to travel. No one can take the journey for you. No one can do your sit-ups for you.

The main thing for me was being kind to myself – having grace for myself. It wasn't easy. The guilt and shame were thick, and I didn't even know how to be kind and gracious to myself. If I wasn't feeling bad, then I would do something to feel bad about or think about something I could feel bad about. There were a lot of different things I could think about to accomplish that, as you well know, having recently read about them.

As you may have noticed, there was some healing that went on during the Impact section, like getting sober (more than once) and going through some counseling for the incest. I believe each of the little steps, even while I was deeply entrenched in distortion and dysfunction, were why I could end up Innocent Again with joy restored. Don't discount the baby steps. It's really all about those small victories. If you don't take the baby steps, how will you ever learn to walk and then run?

Were the first two sections difficult for you to read? Why?

Is being kind and gracious to yourself difficult?

What baby steps have you taken in your journey to healing? (I know one...you are reading this book!)

Relationships Take Work

GOD HAD BEEN a thin thread woven through most of my adult life, but I didn't really have a true relationship with Him. I had always kept Him at a distance, not really knowing Him. I talked to Him, but didn't listen. It was a one-way conversation, like calling someone on the phone, saying everything I want to say, then hanging up. Maybe I didn't want to know what He wanted out of this relationship. Actually, I didn't really understand that He wanted something from me at all! But that's what real relationships are, right? Give and take, talking and listening. My personal relationship with Him was nonexistent. After all, there's no relationship when only one person does the talking. It is a start though. Remember, baby steps…

I invited God to my pity party. I talked to Him when I was drunk, stoned and overeating, basically telling Him, "Look what You've done to me. If You are supposed to know everything about me, then You knew I'd end up here. You knew how terrible the divorce would turn out." My communication was raw and honest. I truly believe that because I invited Him into my mess, He was able to bring me out of it.

That is where I would tell you to start: invite Him into your mess. Don't change a thing, just talk to Him in the middle of it. Talk like you believe He's listening. You do not have to get things in order before you start having a relationship with God. It's not like when you have friends coming over and you clean up your house to make it presentable. God already sees your house the way it is. He wants to be invited in just the way it is. And the best news of all is He will help you clean it. He won't force you to clean it; He helps you want to clean it. It's amazing! It's miraculous! It's joy restored!

Because I wasn't satisfied anymore with just knowing *about* Him and talking to Him, I decided to take our relationship to the next level. I was going to start listening and doing the things I knew I should do: taking the time to know Him. I was going to see if He really could bring joy and peace to my empty life. Just talking to God had brought me only so far, like knowing about a peach by looking at it, learning about it and having others tell me about how it tastes, but never taking a bite.

I was delving in this time…going deep. Doing the work would be worth it. Relationships take work. It was time for me to grow up. I was going to do life on God's terms and see if it worked better than how it had been so far. I was going to renew my mind, reclaim my identity and restore my joy God's way. This renew, reclaim, restore routine would end up becoming a model for an emotional healing course I teach today.

I started purposefully involving God in my everyday life. Each morning, I started my day with Him, reading a daily devotional with Bible scriptures and ten minutes mediating, giving God the time to lay out my day before me. I set an alarm on my phone to remind me morning, noon, and night that God loves me and I am worthy. Listening to a variety of Bible teachers on CD became a new habit. I also went to different Bible studies and did workbooks with homework lessons and went over the answers in small groups. I immersed myself in learning, listening and experiencing God.

Do you believe God can restore your joy?
Do you have a relationship with God?
Do you have a specific God time every day?

Renewing My Mind

I CHOSE TO stop feeling sorry for myself. I chose to stop throwing a pity party and inviting whoever would come to it. I chose to stop the woulda, coulda, shoulda's. What was done was done, and now it was time to get a life. It might not be the life I had planned, but I could still make it a good, good life. It was time to heal.

Another choice I made was to graciously accept myself. I realized I did the best I could at the time. You did the best you could at the time with the information and environment you were in too. *You did the best you could.*

I chose to believe that God loved me. He wasn't punishing me. He had a plan, as it says in Jeremiah 29:11, "For I know the plans I have for you," declares the Lord, "plans to prosper you and not harm you, plans to give you a hope and a future." There wasn't anything I could do to make Him love me more, and there wasn't anything I could do to make Him love me less. I did not need to perform to get God to love me. He loves me. He loves you!

Notice my choice of words above. I didn't say that I **had** to stop feeling sorry for myself, I **had** to stop the woulda, coulda, shoulda's, I **had** to accept myself or I **had** to believe God. I said I **chose** to, and right there is power! I had the power to choose. You have the power to choose. God gave us free will!

This process of renewing my mind was just that…a process. Believe me, it didn't happen overnight. One day when I was revisiting my pity party and feeling sorry for myself (because I lived in an apartment and had no relationship with my kids), I decided to take a walk. By that time, I had learned getting outside could help improve a funky mood. I was talking with (notice *with*, not *to*) God while taking a walk, telling Him about how horrible this situation was and asking what was I supposed to do, hashing out all the woulda, coulda, shoulda's again. Was there something I could do to fix it? I was trying to figure it out, and it was not a good place to be. There was no peace or joy when I let my thinking run amok, reviewing the past, trying to figure out how I could make everything right.

Right then, I noticed a woman across the street pushing a stroller. She had an infant in the stroller and a young child walking alongside her. They were headed to the little city park that was between the multiple apartment complexes in the area.

This next part is difficult to put into words. It was like an instant download from God – a feeling, an awareness, a knowing and an acceptance all at once. I felt like my Daddy (I had started referring to God in that way as I was relating to Him more personally) said, "My child, remember where you were when your children were that age? You lived in that beautiful home in Oregon City with a backyard that had a play structure even better than the one at this city park. It even had a zipline! Remember how you got to stay home with them? Homeschool them? Go camping? Go on vacations? You were blessed."

I was hit with such gratitude. Joy flooded my heart. I knew this feeling was something that could only come from Him. It was instantaneous. Two minutes earlier, joy and gratitude were nowhere to be found. I had tried before to talk myself into gratitude, but this was different. This was a change of heart. My mind was being renewed. I thanked my Daddy for that precious time with my children. I thanked Him for how my wasband had financially made it so I could be home with the kids and homeschool them. We had a big, beautiful, safe yard to play in. I felt so happy for what I had instead of focusing on what was lost.

This was one of the pivotal points in healing for me. I could choose to look at things differently. I

Joy Restored

could choose to see the positive; I could *look* for the positive. My mind was being renewed. I became more grateful. From that day forward, when my thoughts would start going down the hole of feeling sorry for myself, all I had to do was remember that experience. By simply thinking of it, my thoughts could slip right out of pity and into gratitude with ease. Even right now, writing this I think about how grateful I am for the time I had with my kids and I look forward to the day we will be reconciled.

Do you see the difference between have to and choose to?

Do you see how "have to" keeps you a victim and "choose to" gives you power?

Do you recognize that your mind needs to be renewed?

How you can choose to have a different focus, a different frame of reference?

Releasing Guilt

THERE WAS ONE particular Bible teacher who I started learning a lot from. She helped me so much in my walk with God. She was also sexually abused by her dad, so we had similar distortions to work through. I was listening to one of her CDs where she admitted she used to feel guilty if she didn't feel guilty. I totally understood what she meant. I had been so riddled with guilt for so long. If I didn't feel guilty, then I would do something to feel guilty about. It's like feeling guilty was an obligation. The Lord revealed that to me in a profound way, helping me release my guilt.

I was driving to work one morning and it was raining really hard. I figured I could speed because no police officer would want to pull someone over in this downpour! As I was speeding along, a police car passed me. He turned on his lights and did a quick little siren blast as he cruised past. I was so racked with guilt that I pulled over. The police car pulled over then too, in front of me, at least five car lengths away, and the officer came running back to me in the rain. I rolled down my window and he yelled at me, "DO YOU WANT A TICKET?" I started crying and said, "No." He yelled, "THEN WHY DID YOU PULL OVER?" I said through tears, "I was speeding." He yelled, "I DIDN'T PULL YOU OVER! I DIDN'T COME IN BEHIND YOU! I PASSED YOU AND GAVE YOU A FLASH OF MY LIGHTS AND A QUICK LITTLE SIREN AS A WARNING TO SLOW DOWN, NOT PULL OVER!" Then he marched off back to his vehicle.

I sat there for a while stunned, trying to figure out what just happened. I didn't understand that I didn't need to pull over. The policeman's words were repeating in my mind. "I didn't pull you over." Then why *did* I pull over? Another one of those instant downloads from my Daddy came, like when I saw the lady in the park with her young kids. A feeling, an awareness, a knowing and an acceptance all at once happened more and more in my life as I was developing an intimate relationship with Him.

This time it was like He said, "My child, you have so much guilt and shame that it causes you to make wrong choices, take wrong actions. You do things you don't even need to do. You take actions you don't need to take. You may have done something wrong, but you carry that wrong too far. You hold onto it too long and it affects your vision, your doing, your being. This has been an issue most of your life and we are going to fix that. You have behaved in ways that were driven by guilt and shame. As you continue to grow in your understanding of how much I love you, you won't be driven by guilt or shame, but by My love." This was another pivotal point in my healing. This time, I felt a new level of forgiveness for myself. It was so freeing! And so necessary to restoring joy!

Do you feel an inappropriate sense of guilt?

Do you know you can be set free from guilt?

Seeing Differently

MY DADDY STARTED revealing to me how He saw femininity and sexuality. This was (and is) a big project. Even if a woman hasn't been sexually abused, she is abused by our Western culture of sexualizing women. I could get on such a soapbox right now. It could be a whole book! I even know what I would call it: *Femininity Distorted*. But I digress…

There were several ways God opened my eyes to this complex issue. The main one that brought me onto the path of restoring my femininity was a conversation with my upstairs neighbor. We ended up on the topic of a popular talent show. When she told me, she watched it, I was shocked. She was a very Spirit-filled woman. Like me, she also referred to God as "Daddy". She had a rich, personal walk with Him, and I felt blessed to have her as my neighbor. I knew it was a gift from our Daddy for each of us!

She could see the shock and judgement on my face when she said she watched it with her husband and son.

I said, "I don't understand how you can even watch that. It's all about sexualizing women in their scantily-dressed outfits."

She looked back at me just as shocked and judging. How could I see an innocent talent show as sexualizing women? Those women were beautiful and talented. How sad for me that I couldn't see that, and only saw a woman being sexualized. It was one of those downloads again. An out of body experience…a time warp.

In that moment, I got to see the world from her eyes; eyes that hadn't been distorted to femininity the way mine had. It was freeing. It was like a gift. "Here My child, you too can see the world like this – the way I designed the world to be before the distortion. These women are beautiful, talented, strong, committed, and feminine." It was another glimpse of being Innocent Again. The world didn't need to be seen through sexual glasses. I wanted more of this new view! A whole new path had been revealed to me. I liked it. I was going to walk down it and see where it led.

I started deliberately looking at things with new eyes. If I didn't have the past that I had, how would I see this? How could it be seen differently? What is the way it's supposed to be seen? How did my Creator design it? What was His plan before all the distortion?

Don't get me wrong here – there are definitely things that are wrong no matter how you look at them. But I had been taught to see things sexually. I could turn the most innocent thing into a sexual thing. My thinking was distorted, which leads to distorted seeing, which leads to distorted doing. Becoming Innocent Again made me so excited. How do you view femininity?

Do you feel like it has been distorted by your past or society?

Living in the Moment

I HEARD A great sermon about having no past. It had a huge impact on me. The God download happened again. And when I say download, I mean more than realizing it in my brain or learning something. These go much deeper. I instantly feel it, like it's a reality. If I could truly believe I had no past, that I was forgiven, then in this moment I was free to be whoever I wanted to be.

From then on, I started living in the moment, letting go of the woulda, coulda, shoulda's on a deeper level and believing I was free to move forward without the baggage. I started watching for all of the ways God was moving in my life. I stopped believing the lies about myself and started seeing myself and others through God's eyes.

While learning to apply this truth of having no past and being free to enjoy the moment, I was driving to visit my mom at her store. Nothing out of the ordinary was going on. It was a nice day with blue skies. One of my favorite Christian songs came on the radio and I started singing along with it. Then, this feeling started coming over me.

I remember exactly where I was, heading into a major intersection in town. Out of nowhere, the strongest feeling of joy came over me, like this was the greatest moment in my life. It was so strange! I felt like I was about to burst with gratitude. Everything looked brighter and sounded clearer. A fleeting thought of *am I about to die?* crossed my mind as I pulled through the intersection. Was I going to be in a big accident and be taken to Heaven? I continued through the intersection, singing, crying and feeling a joy that was beyond my intellect. It made no sense.

As the feeling became less intense, my Daddy said to me (impressed on my heart), "That is what living in the moment is. You were experiencing the now. Right now is all you have. The present is where I am. I want you to experience more of these moments. I have given you the ability to create them. Stop. Slow down. Live in the moment you are in. Feel the moment. No past, no future, just right now. That is the moment *I live in*."

When my pity party thoughts and attitude would try to return, it was my signal to stop and concentrate on the right-now moment. Every time I would stop my stinking thinking and focus on the moment,

I would realize that everything in the moment was okay. All was well. I was able to restore joy moment by moment!

After that, I intentionally practiced being in the moment. *Right now, in this very moment, I have everything I need. This moment is perfect.* I started being joyful living in my small apartment. I started being joyful driving my used 2003 Kia minivan. I started being joyful being broke. I started being joyful in my obese body. I started being joyful that I had kids, even if I didn't see them. Joy was being restored. I became joyful. Those moments grew into minutes, turned into hours, and then turned into days, weeks, months and years.

My circumstances didn't make me joyful; choosing to see life from my Daddy's perspective did. Being grateful did. Seeing the blessings all around me did. Stopping feeling sorry for myself and renewing my mind did. This is not a one and done thing, however. It is ongoing. It doesn't mean I am always in joy, but it does mean I can always find joy. And so can you!

Does finding joy moment by moment seem unrealistic?

Would you be willing to give it a chance?

Would you be willing to work for it?

Wouldn't Change a Thing

JAMES 1:2-4 SAYS, "Consider it pure joy, my brothers and sisters, whenever you face trials of many kinds, because you know that the testing of your faith produces perseverance. Let perseverance finish its work so than you may be mature and complete, not lacking anything." I have become that person; I lack nothing. My circumstances are not why I feel this way. I feel this way because I know who I am. The person I have become would not have happened without the struggle.

Once again, my Daddy gave me one of those instant downloads to solidify this truth for me. Through my process of healing God did bring into my life a wonderful man who I did marry, which is a great story for another time.My new husband's job took him to Eugene for a trade show and I went with him. I wanted to see my old stomping grounds, the University of Oregon, where I attended college for four terms. A fascinating revelation hit me while I was there.

Mike and I were standing on the sidewalk in front of my first dorm room; the sidewalk where I would have walked hundreds of times going to and from classes. I was filled with so much joy in that moment, thinking about how blessed I was, how happily remarried I was. God said, "Do you really feel that way?"

Then He popped an image into my head of my younger self walking towards me, like she was coming back from a class to her dorm room. It was surreal. He said, "Now's your chance. You can say something to her as she passes by you. You will only have a moment. What will you say to her?"

She was moving towards me. My brain was racing trying to figure out what I should say. *Don't marry The Wasband? Don't have kids? Don't move to Sauvie Island?* She was getting closer...I didn't have much time. I remembered how, just a moment ago, I had been feeling so full of joy with where I was in my life. She was one step away.

Would saying something now to my younger self end up with me not arriving at where I was now? Would I miss out on having the intimate relationship I have with my Daddy (which is the best thing that ever happened to me)? In that moment, I realized

Joy Restored

I really wouldn't change anything. If having what I had with God meant walking through all of what I walked through, I wouldn't change a thing. As she walked past me, I turned and said, "It's all going to work out," and watched her walk away knowing it was 100% true!

Conclusion

It is going to all work out for you too! "And we know that all things work together for good to those who love God, to those who are called according to His purpose." Romans 8:28.

New beginnings are for *everyone*! "Therefore, if anyone is in Christ, the new creation has come: The old has gone, the new is here." 2 Corinthians 5:17.

We can renew our minds, change our thinking and change our behavior. It all starts with the mind. It is scientifically proven that we can rewire our brains – it's called neuroplasticity. God calls it renewing your mind (Romans 12:2).

We weren't meant to be miserable in this life, barely getting by, hurting, stuck in our pasts. God does not want that for us. We were created to have the abundant life: a life of joy and peace. Jesus even says it Himself; He came so that we could have an abundant life (John 10:10). I am living proof of joy restored, of

God's amazing grace. I pray that by learning about some of my story, you can see that abundant life and joy can be true for you too!

At the time of writing this book, I am moving into my ninth year of sobriety. I live in a cute little house that backs up to a wildlife sanctuary. I drive my dream car. I am healthy and fit. I travel to tropical places. I have a Finntastic (my last name is Finn) marriage. I am so full of peace and joy it's overflowing. I truly want to help you have that too! It can be yours.

If you or someone you know has been sexually abused, please share my story with them. I have also created some special resources to help survivors move from victim to victor. The journey of healing shouldn't be taken alone. I would be honored to take it with you. Let's get incest and childhood sexual abuse out of the closet! Let's shine light into the darkness!

Please reach out to me via email at journeytoinnocentagain@gmail.com.

Visit my website www.innocentagain.com.

Also, join me at my Facebook page https://www.facebook.com/renewreclaimrestore/ and let's create a movement!

Renew, Reclaim, Restore! No more secrets! Remember, we can become #innocentagain and help others do the same!

CPSIA information can be obtained
at www.ICGtesting.com
Printed in the USA
FSHW020434240520
70409FS